An Invitation to
Pause...again

An Invitation To Pause...again

Published by Blue Bungalow Press

ISBN 978-0-578-60614-9

Cover photo
Freedom by guvendemr

*Cover and Interior Design
by Ellen Klempner-Béguin*

Edited by Jeremy Brown

Printed in the United States of America

An Invitation to Pause...again

musings from a mindfulness coach
about life and dementia

by Janet Archer

For My Mom

Little did I know, that in the end,
you would be one of my greatest teachers.
I love how life always gives us
what we need most.
And life gave me you.

It was four years ago that I published *An Invitation to Pause: musings from a mindfulness teacher*. I have had the time of my life traveling, speaking and sharing those stories with hundreds of people from all over the world.

An Invitation to Pause...again, is a continuation of my meanderings and musings of life, liberally sprinkled with more stories of my mom Frannie, who has been traveling down the road of dementia for the last eight years.

We are all in this journey of humanness together. Even though my musings are personal, my hope is that you recognize yourself on these pages and celebrate with both tears and laughter the preciousness of this one life that you have been given.

May this book be a gift for your soul.

Janet Archer
October 21, 2019

Contents

Back in the Saddle

Me on my front porch swing, NH 2016

I pulled into the parking lot, turned off the car and decided to bring only my wallet with me into the store.

No cell phone, no big bag weighing my shoulder down.

I was feeling very buoyant, having just left a fun book reading party with some fabulous women.

When I got to the checkout, there was someone ahead of me who was needing price checks on five or six items.

Instead of standing there watching the whole long process and getting irritated that it was taking so long, I decided to tidy up my wallet.

My turn came. I paid for my items and went out to my car.

Walking to the car, listening to the click, click, click of my uncomfortable dress boots on the pavement, I noticed that the air had gotten cooler and I was getting cold because my coat was tucked away in the back seat of my car.

My feet hurt, I was growing cold. I could not wait to get home and put my feet up in my nice warm house.

When I arrived at the car, I just stood there and wondered:

where the heck were my keys?

No pockets, no pocketbook, no coat, no anything but my wallet.

Just me on the outside of the car wanting everything I could see in the inside of the car!

After a bit, I leaned my head in towards the window one more time, willing my car to open.

And viola, just like that, the car lights went on and that familiar click of the door opening was like music to my ears.

I was not surprised that the car door opened.

I was expecting a miracle and here it was.

The last three words I read at the book reading party were ANYTHING IS POSSIBLE.

I was giddy with delight as I now sat on the inside looking out.

I started dancing and singing and screaming with joy.

After a few minutes of bouncing around in my car, it slowly dawned on me;

I still had no idea where my car keys were.

This was certainly some bit of crazy.

I could not stop laughing.

And neither could the man from the store.

He had followed me out of the store at a big distance, clicked my car open and then watched the crazy woman dance and scream for a bit before he handed over the keys (which I had left on the counter when I cleaned out my wallet).

He was clearly happy with himself, grinning ear to ear as he stood outside my window dangling the keys in his hand.

His joke on me had made my already wonderful day fantastic!

Since I published the book *An Invitation to Pause* some months earlier, I had not written one single word. Nothing.

I had lots of excuses why.

But in that moment, sitting in my car, none of that mattered because when he handed me those keys, I knew without a doubt that he also handed me this story to be written.

So here I am. I'm back, and it feels great to be back in the saddle once again.

Remember this my dear readers:

No matter where you are or what you are doing, if you expect the doors to open, then they most certainly will.

Fleetingly Precious

This day has never been here before and will never come again.

This is the moment you have been waiting for.

Quench your thirst and live like there is no tomorrow.

Sing and dance and stick your head out the window.

Look around. Smile. Give. Receive. Open. Allow.

Get out of the stories that don't serve you, the ones that are parading around in your head pretending to be so important and urgent.

Feel the breeze on your face.

Life is happening all around and through you.

Let it tingle you alive today.

All of this, what we call our life,

is so fleetingly precious.

The Milkshake

I always order her the same thing:

cheeseburger, fries and a medium chocolate milkshake.

We were at McDonald's for lunch - my mom's favorite.

When we woke up at my mom's house four years ago to find that my stepfather had died in the night, I asked my mom what I could do for her.

"Get me a chocolate milkshake from McDonald's," was her answer.

I got her the largest one they had and watched her nurse it all morning long as she sat with the shock of having lost her second husband.

She absolutely loves those chocolate milkshakes and I wanted to make sure that she got a delicious chocolate milkshake on that day. I wanted her to be happy.

When the girl from behind the counter brought our tray to the table, I stared at the milkshake.

There was nothing chocolate about it; it was totally white!

I picked it up and asked the girl why it wasn't brown.

She told me that they had run out of chocolate syrup and the machine was down. She promised to bring my mother another one when they had it fixed.

My mom likes everything to be as she expects it to be.

What I came to find out sitting there in McDonald's on that fine morning was SO DO I.

I was worried that she would freak out.

I decided not to tell her about what was going on. I put the straw in and sent the drink over to her side of the table.

She took a sip and then another.

I asked her if she was enjoying her milkshake and she nodded yes.

Meanwhile, I wasn't enjoying any of it. I was fuming that the girl, after ten minutes, had not brought over another milkshake for my mom, the one she WANTED, the chocolate one.

I could see that the machine had been fixed, as people were ordering and drinking their chocolate milkshakes all over the place.

Happy people with their happy chocolate milkshakes!

I wanted to jump over the counter, push the girl aside and make the shake myself.

I was making myself miserable.

Then I looked over at my mom again. She had been busily eating her food and drinking her shake.

In fact, the shake was almost gone. It was then that she smiled at me, pointed to her vanilla shake and said, "GOOD!"

All along, she had been one of those happy people drinking their happy shakes.

My mind had been going 220 miles per hour on a track of dissatisfaction. I almost missed what was right in front of me because I was so consumed with the conversation in my head.

There was my mom, sitting across from me, smiling.

Chocolate, vanilla, she didn't care. Why was I holding on so tight?

I let go.

As we got up to leave, I walked over to the girl behind the cash register and said, "Thank you so much."

I love when life gives you exactly what you need, and when some of your best lessons can come from a milkshake!

It's Time

The Original Mantel Clock- 2016

I grew up with a mantel clock that tick-tocked every minute of every day and then struck the appropriate number of gongs on every hour.

I never liked the clock.

I'm a silence kind of gal and the tick-tocking drove me a little insane.

Later, when my mom moved away from our family home, she took the clock with her and set it up in the guest/den room, which is where I slept when I visited.

She knew to stop the clock from ticking when I got there and then wind it back up when I left.

Somehow, that clock has landed in the back of my car.

When we moved my mom in September, we had to clean out her apartment.

By that time, she had long since stopped winding up the clock or even caring that she had a clock.

So, the clock went into the back of my car and was soon forgotten, until this morning.

I went over a big bump and the clock started gonging and I heard myself say,

"IT'S TIME for me to get that clock out of the back of the car!"

A flood gate of thoughts about time opened up in my mind.

What else is it time for?

Maybe it's time for me to actually start drinking green drinks instead of saying that I want to drink green drinks - or else it's time to stop saying that this is what I want to do and then do nothing about it.

Big or small, it doesn't matter.

I know

that you know

that it's time

for something.

The minutes are ticking and the hours are gonging.

What is it time for in your life?

Time for joy, compassion, freedom, health, patience, honesty?

Time to clean out something, dig into something?

Time to get to know the person who resides inside you or beside you?

Time to forgive? Forget? Remember? Move on? Move in?

Time to live lightly, live loudly?

Well my friend,

IT IS TIME.

What will it be?

The Scarf

Me wearing the scarf- 2015

When I roll up my yoga mat, I wrap it with a beautifully colored scarf of pinks, blues, yellows and white.

This scarf was a present that was given to me by an amazing woman a few years ago.

That amazing woman was my friend.

And my friend was dying.

I remember the day so well. I was hosting a pool party at an indoor pool.

It was the third annual and she had been to both the first and second. We expected that she wouldn't make it to this one because she was so sick.

But there she was, walking through the door with a huge smile on her face, yelling, "I wouldn't miss this for anything. Let's get this party started!"

That day we all remembered what it was like to play like children - relay races with balloons shoved under water-soaked tight t-shirts, where we raced to chairs so we could pop more balloons with our butts, which it turned out, was not an easy feat.

Laughing as we pulled each other off of those big, long noodles, squirting each other with squirt guns and singing loudly to my special pool-party play list that was blasting in the background.

Grown women totally abandoning any beliefs about how one should behave in midlife.

Even with all that fun and lightness, the highlight of the day for me was my friend being there fully alive, even as the huge weight of death hung over her - hung over all of us.

Oh, my heart was broken wide open knowing that this laughing with her would be the last time.

When we were leaving, she pulled out from her bag the most beautiful scarf of pinks, blues, yellows and white and gave it to me saying, "This is for you. I thought you would really love this."

My heart stopped beating, even though she was the one dying.

That moment felt so powerfully raw.

So intimate, so very, very real.

This is what it is like to be human, to live this human experience with the full range of emotions that we are each designed to feel, emotions that feel like they will kill us. But they will not.

I did not want to back away from the intensity of that moment.

I chose to lock my eyes with hers and accept what she was offering me, a piece of her, a remembrance, a sweetness that I could wrap myself up in and carry with me for as long as my days last.

Life.

It is amazingly raw.

And we humans?

We are so amazingly strong.

The Lunch Date

Dylan's 1st birthday party

"Why are we here?" she asks me with what I detect to be a bit of an edge to her voice.

I am opening the car door for my mother so I can help her get out to go into the restaurant to eat her favorite soup that she just told me ten minutes ago that she wanted.

It's raining.

I'm not in a good mood.

I ignore the fact that she doesn't want to be here and claims that she never wanted soup.

I assist her out of the car. We go into the restaurant, sit down, order and wait.

The soup comes and she refuses to eat it.

My mom says, "You need to get your mind checked. You need to get some common sense into that brain of yours."

Ten minutes after we enter, we leave the restaurant with two soups in doggie bags.

30 minutes after starting out on our lunch date, my mom is back in her room, telling me to go home.

That is exactly what I do.

I go home, sit down and eat both of those soups.

I realized that I do need to check my mind or, better yet, I need to keep my mind in check!

My mind that sometimes insists that everything needs to be a certain way and can take things very personally.

What I run up against is that in the world of dementia, nothing is certain.

The road map changes constantly.

And when it does, I am left lost and confused each and every time that I forget to "use my common sense," as my mother calls it.

It's only when I can manage my own mind and remember that I am not in control of either my mother or her disease, that I can find humor in the situation, not take any of it personally and fully enjoy every last drop of those delicious soups!

Here and There

HERE &
THERE

If you take the T away from the word There, you get the word Here.

Here and There are really very similar to the eye and yet they are so extremely far apart in reality.

As a culture, we are taught to strive for There.

"When I get There, all my problems will be solved and life will be so much better."

But every time we get There, it is like the proverbial carrot dangling in front of us; there is always a new There to get to.

If we are always trying to get There and not dropping down into Here while getting to There, we are out ahead of ourselves and missing the joy of living in the Here.

Being Here has to be practiced every day.

You can't get Here if you are always practicing getting There.

In the rush and tumble of everyday life, drop the T as many times as you can and get to Here.

Because at the end of our lives, we will finally realize that there was no There.

There was only ever

This. Here. Now.

Driving With the Top Down

About fifteen years ago, I had an experience that I had totally forgotten about until yesterday. I was doing some serious resting and relaxing at one of my favorite yoga centers when a vision of what happened came floating through my awareness.

I was at a workshop. One person was invited up to the stage. She was asked to silently think of something and then those of us in the audience were asked to notice what arose in our own minds as she was doing this. We were also asked not to censor what we saw or felt, no matter how ridiculous.

Ridiculous it was.

What I saw seemed utterly silly.

It made no sense to me.

I was actually embarrassed to say what I saw.

Then it was my turn.

"I saw a woman, a beautiful woman, wearing a scarf on her head tied at her neck. She had a cigarette in one of those long cigarette holders. Her one hand was holding the cigarette and the other was on the wheel of a car, a convertible with the top down. She appeared to me to be full of life and joy. She seemed very happy, very at peace with herself in this snapshot moment.

My turn passed as others began reporting what they saw or felt. The woman on the stage remained stone silent. She gave no response to anyone.

When we had all shared, the teacher asked her to tell us what she had been thinking about.

She told us that she had been thinking about the last time she saw her mother alive.

Her mother had driven off with a scarf wrapped around her head, a cigarette in her hand and the top to the convertible down.

She had an accident two miles down the road.

The daughter had carried thoughts about the terror of the accident around in her heart and not remembered the joy and happiness of her very alive mother. She had shut down too much of her life from that point forward.

My willingness to participate and to swim in some embarrassment was such an amazing gift to this woman.

I have no reason to explain why I saw so clearly what I saw that day. I just did.

The Gift from the Gift?

Perhaps it is that we can all intend to be there for each other and encourage each other to drive our convertibles with the top down while we can, since we never know what may be waiting for us two miles down the road.

SIRI to the Rescue

I had just gotten out of an appointment and was getting ready to drive home.

I had it all planned. I was going to listen to a podcast that I had saved and been excited about hearing.

It was going to be wonderful.

I dug my hand into my bag to get the cord for the phone.

I began pulling out tangled earbuds, cords that went to everything but the phone, rubber bands, lost lipsticks and tons of notes to myself.

When I finally found what I was looking for, I realized that the plug didn't fit. But that didn't stop me. I kept plugging that plug into the opening that it didn't fit into over and over, while getting madder and madder. I was bordering on manic.

That is when I heard a loud voice come out of my own mouth yelling,

"WHAT IS WRONG WITH YOU JANET?"

It reverberated through the car and landed heavily in my heart and on my lap.

But then, and this is the best thing ever, I heard a woman's voice with a British accent respond;

"NOT A THING!"

It was SIRI from my iPhone.

In all my muddling, pulling, punching and plugging in, I must have turned her on.

I have heard it said that technology is taking us away from being present in the world.

But on this day, SIRI brought me smack dab back to the moment, back to myself.

The hijacking in my head was over.

I was calm and more than a bit blown away by SIRI's enlightening remark.

Just for fun, I pushed the SIRI button and said, "Thank you. You are amazing,"

To which she replied,

"I am putting myself to the fullest possible use, which is all I think any conscious entity can ever hope to do. You really don't need to thank me!"

Seriously,

I do believe that SIRI has gone a bit ZEN.

The Joy of Pete

My mom and Pete, 2015

I got my mom a talking parrot.

Not a real one, but a colorful fake one that is sitting on a perch.

When you turn him on, he flaps his wings and repeats what you say.

Pete, the repeating parrot.

I got the idea from a dementia website. They had a video of a woman with dementia talking to her parrot. She sat right in front of the parrot and was having a conversation with it. She was very happily engaged. I was both impressed and interested.

I wondered if this could be a possibility for my mom.

My mom who doesn't like to talk to anyone.

My mom who likes to glare and criticize.

A conversation to her is telling people, in her opinion, what they need to change or fix.

I had no idea how my mom would respond.

But what if she did respond like the woman in the video? That would be pretty cool.

So, I plunked the $13.00 down and came home with Pete.

The smile on her face when he first talked was worth the price alone.

Even my mom, the armored woman, melted in the presence of this fake, multi-colored new friend.

Pete wasn't interested in carrying on a conversation about anything that my mom could no longer understand. Just like her, he liked to say things over and over again. He showed neither judgment nor impatience towards her. He was clearly the perfect companion.

She calls him Pretty Pete and then she laughs.

He says back to her, Pretty Pete and then he laughs.

She laughs, he laughs, she laughs more, he laughs more.

And so it goes.

How long will it last?

Who knows and who cares?

Right now, in this moment on this day, there is a friendship blooming and laughs erupting.

Joy has hit assisted living, and this joy has the colors of the rainbow on its big beautiful wings.

You never know what is going to fly into your life, soothe your soul and make you laugh out loud.

How fantastically great is that!

The Nest

We have a beauty bush on the south side of the house.

I love having the expanse of branches and leaves and the brilliant pink explosion of color in the spring that I can look out at from six different windows.

That's a lot of beauty bush, and a lovely home for two baby cardinals who just arrived last week.

I noticed the adult male first, brilliant red, flitting around the bush, talking to the female who spoke back every time he called.

I climbed up on chairs and looked out every window until I found her nest, with two tiny eggs in it, right below my upstairs closet window.

It was such joy, watching every day as the eggs turned into baby birds who held their mouths wide open waiting to be fed.

I could peer down into their throats, watch their hearts beating and feel the coziness of the two little ones nested tightly next to each other.

I watched as the days flowed into nights, as rain pelted down and then the sun shone brightly, and as the wind alternately blew mightily and then became still.

Through it all, the mom and dad took care of the babies and each other.

The little ones grew and flourished and their hearts kept beating and their mouths kept opening to be fed.

I couldn't help but feel that I had been allowed to take part in something incredibly private and sacred.

One day, as I watched from the upstairs window, the female cardinal looked up at me and we caught each other's eye.

I froze, relaxed my body and sent an energetic message to her:

"Thank you for allowing me to take part in your miracle out here in the bush. I am not here to harm any of you. I feel so blessed by your presence and would consider it an honor if you continued to allow me to drop in from time to time. Having your family here is such a gift for me."

She must have given her consent because as I worked on my computer, the male sang to me outside my window, the female followed me around the garden and the worms gave up their lives for the babies in the nest.

I got to watch the whole show!

I am sitting on a plane at this moment. I left this morning and right as the plane was taking off with its big airplane wings spread wide, I realized that I had forgotten to say goodbye to the family of cardinals.

When I arrive home in a week, the babies will probably be gone along with the mother and father.

At some point we all fly off to somewhere.

Everything changes.

And sometimes we forget our roots.

We were all fed, or else we would not have survived our youth.

Our hearts all still beat, otherwise we would not be here to read this right now.

We were all once babies in the nest before we took flight into the big wide world.

And even though we are out in this big wide world, we will always be of the nest.

The beating of your heart and my heart and the cardinals' hearts is nothing other than the rhythm and music of life.

Feeding ourselves and each other is the thread of connection that is woven between us, much like the threads of a nest which are securely fastened to withstand anything.

No matter how many times we fly away, no matter how far we go, we can always, always find our way home, back into the coziness of this enormous nest we call life.

There is room here for us all.

The Right Place to Look

Have you heard the story about the woman who loses her car keys?

She loses them in her living room.

It's night and all the lights are off in the room, so she doesn't know exactly where they fell.

Just then a street light goes on outside.

She gathers her things and goes out to look for her car keys under the beam of the shining street light.

A neighbor comes by and starts to help her look.

After a bit, the neighbor asks her exactly where she lost the keys.

"In my living room," she replies.

You probably agree with me that this is a silly story. Of course she wouldn't go outside to find the keys that she lost in her living room.

But.....this is what we do in our minds. We step out of ourselves to find the answer that we can only find within.

I'm doing it right now; looking under that darn street lamp.

As I sit here writing, I am jumping up and down from my chair to move wind chimes around on branches to get the best sound I can with the wind that is blowing outside.

I've got one eye on the clock, knowing that I am behind the schedule I set for myself and worrying about how I am going to get this done plus everything else I wanted to do today.

As my attention is split and clearly not focused on the one task at hand, I accidentally delete everything I had written for the last hour and can't find it anywhere in the trash.

I want to blame everybody and everything and make the fault for what is happening at this moment lie outside of myself.

I don't want to stop and turn on my own light to see what is happening inside, what thoughts might be lurking in there that are creating my unease.

But in the end, this is what I do.

I turn the light on and have a look around.

And, in the looking, I find, face to face, a woman who has a sincere intention to keep her commitments but who is afraid she can't.

A woman who sometimes forgets that it is the journey itself and not the destination that is of the most importance.

In daring to look, to stop and shine the light of awareness on myself, I begin to feel everything inside shifting.

"I'm 50 minutes behind schedule" becomes "If I hadn't been here at this exact moment, I would not have seen the heron fly by over the water just now."

"I lost my first draft" becomes "That's OK, If I hadn't lost it, I wouldn't have had the pleasure of writing this second version which is so different from the first."

I'm glad I turned my own light on, so I could find what I was looking for.

Right now, in this moment, as I watch the tide of the river floating by, I can feel myself swimming in the joy of well-being, and that happens to be so worth the small effort that it took to flick the switch.

Me in the hammock, NC, 2018

Love in a Wagon

Rex, San Francisco, 2017

I'd like you to meet Rex.

He's a pug from San Francisco.

He goes for walks down the beach boardwalk in his bright red Radio Flyer.

He barks at all the dogs running by him.

He turns himself around and around on his butt as he lets everyone know he is there, he is a fighter and he has still got some life left to live.

Rex can't walk; he's paralyzed.

He has had several operations for which his odds of surviving were very low.

But survive them he did. Every day he enjoys this ritual where he announces to the world, "Hey, it's Rex. I'm still here. I'm still in the game."

Rex's person, the man who pulls the wagon, is madly in love with his dog. You can see that he would do anything for him.

Meeting them on this day got me thinking.

When and if I need a wagon, I hope it is big and red and that my people on the other end of the handle bring me out so I can continue to be part of this world that I so love.

If I am feeling like I want to hide out and feel sorry for myself, I hope they will ignore me and just sit my butt down in that wagon anyway, knowing that the sunshine and the connection to all you other dogs out there will heal my soul.

And if you happen to be the one who needs to be pulled around, please ask me, because it would bring me great joy to know that I am assisting you in finding happiness.

I think in the end it doesn't matter if you're the one with the hand on the handle or the butt in the seat, because without each other, it just doesn't work.

Side by Side

Me and my mom in a rain shower, Hawaii, 2010

I discovered something so simple and amazing today.
It was calming for me and, I project, for my mother too.

I call it the "side by side."

My mother seems comforted with me by her side, not in front of her, not talking at her and not looking into her eyes trying to find that spark of the woman she was.

She relaxes with me by her side.

We are on the back porch.

She has her feet up on the ottoman while sitting in the rocking chair.

I am next to her at the table on my computer writing.

We sit like this for hours, her watching the birds and the insects on the screen and me lost in writing.

Every once in a while, she looks over and excitedly questions me about what I am doing. "Are you a writer? Have you really written a book? When will I see it?"

Pleased with my answers, she goes back to rocking and I go back to typing.

Hours later, we go out to dinner and I sit across from her.

She stares at me for a long time.

She looks upset and then she says,

"Why do you let your bangs grow so long? You look awful! You need to cut those bangs. What is the matter with you, looking like that?"

My mother was always in charge of my bangs while I was growing up. She would grab the scissors and cut my bangs so unevenly that I was embarrassed to leave the house for days.

In this moment, at the restaurant, she is back in my childhood as the mother demanding her daughter's bangs get cut.

I laugh and tell her that we will get the scissors later when I take her home and then she can cut my bangs.

Satisfied, she goes back to drinking her iced tea, mumbling about how bad I look.

She will not remember the bangs or the scissors by the time we go home, so I am not worried about my hair. I am though, very curious.

After such a wonderful afternoon together, just happy being together side by side out on the porch, why did she all of a sudden notice my bangs and get so upset?

So, I ask her.

The simplicity of her answer astounds me;

"I didn't see you when you weren't sitting right in front of me."

Profound and the absolute truth.

I've given my mom my arm to hold and my shoulder to lean on as she moves more deeply into this disease.

And now I know for sure that being there by her side is the best place to be for both of us.

Emma and Jamie, Sunset Beach, NC, 2019

The Balancing Squirrel

Most people tend to hold their breath when they practice a balance pose in a yoga class.

Muscles tighten and jaws clench just because they are attempting to stand on one foot or the other.

Thoughts like, "I've got to be able to do this, I'll look like a fool if I fall, why don't I have better balance and this is way too hard," seem to flood the mind and nothing but a ton of tension is created.

Creating more tension in an already tight body is not really the point when practicing yoga.

What if we used balance practice as an opportunity not to give up on ourselves?

Maybe we could take on a "so what" attitude.

I might fall, so what.

I'm falling, so what.

I fell, so what.

I'll be a cheater if I leave a foot on the floor or hold the wall. Really? Who says so and anyway, so what.

Why do we use so many opportunities to make ourselves wrong, to set a high bar of perfection that we might never reach and along the way, as we are trying to reach that perfection, we get really tense and usually give up on ourselves?

The other day I watched a squirrel climb a bush outside my window and then try to hop from a branch in the bush over to a bird feeder that sat in the middle of the lawn. They were very far away from each other.

That squirrel was not about to give up.

I sat and watched him for quite a long time and before long, he nailed it.

He jumped from the bush to the roof of the bird feeder where he landed flat on his feet.

I really didn't think he was going to be able to do it.

I wanted to go out and shake his hand and tell him that I was so impressed with his perseverance and that I admired his style.

I had counted how many times he tried and DIDN'T make it to the bird feeder.

17 TIMES. And that is not counting the times he tried to climb the bird feeder pole, only to be greeted with the squirrel shield that stopped him every time.

He never gave up on himself. He kept choosing to go back again and again until finally he landed right where he wanted to be.

Jump. Fall. Get up. Repeat.

Over and over.

It's like balancing in yoga class.

Balance. Lose balance. Get up. Repeat.

Granted, he was looking for food to sustain him and fill his belly.

But aren't we looking for something to sustain us when we practice yoga?

Next time you are about to "jump" into a balance pose, channel some squirrel energy.

Make the choice not to give up on yourself.

Relax into that powerful moment of not caring whether you fall or not.

Feel everything soften as you take a breather from taking yourself so darn seriously.

Be like the squirrel.

It looks to me like it would be so much more fun!

The Quarter Turn

Church steeple, NH 2017

It was early one morning when I was out for a walk that a brightness caught my eye.

"What is that?" I wondered as I backed up to investigate.

There was a cross on a church steeple, shining with a spectacular brilliance, which proved to be nothing more than a reflection of the newly risen sun.

Later in the day, I was in my car when I realized I had forgotten my cell phone. I had left it at home on the table.

"I can't believe I forgot my cell phone!" I started yelling. "What if I need it later? What if I miss something important?"

I was stirring myself up at a frightening speed.

That's when I remembered the cross and the sun from earlier in the day and I asked myself, "What are you facing right now, Janet? Are you facing the sun?"

Quite simply, the answer was NO.

I was facing agitation, worry and anger straight on - and that is what got reflected back to me.

When I made the choice to take a quarter turn toward the sun, this is what it sounded like in my head:

"How relaxing not to have my phone. Nobody can reach me right now except me.

59

I wonder what I most need to hear from myself that would assist and support me along the way today?"

It's always our choice what direction we face.

Face the sun, the light, kindness, gratitude and willingness and it will all be reflected back, each and every time.

Look out from where you are and you will absolutely know, in a very short time, just what direction you are facing.

If you don't like the reflection, just start to turn and don't stop until you feel the glow spread across your face and slide down into your heart.

And then, welcome yourself back home, once again, into your own sweet brilliance.

What Do I Do?

"What do I do?" asked my mother.

I had just helped her out of the car. She was standing there in the parking lot completely confused. I took her arm and led her inside as I explained where we were and why we were there.

Not four weeks earlier, I had heard myself say those very same words, "What do I do?" as I stood in a different parking lot.

My mom had not taken any of her medication for four days. She would spit it out along with her water while aiming for anyone in her sight. By the time I saw her, she was raging, trying to bite, push, kick or hit anyone who got close enough to her. She was like what I would imagine a rabid dog to be like. I was frightened by the intensity of the wildness. The nurses thought I might be able to find an inroad, but they were mistaken. I was of no help. I felt like I was drowning in my own "please don't make this be happening" thoughts.

I don't want to know the particulars of how someone was actually able to get close enough to get her into an ambulance and take her to the hospital. They had asked me to meet her there, so I drove my own car over and missed whatever had transpired.

When I walked into the emergency room, the first thing I noticed was that four men were struggling to hold my mom down on the bed, two at her wrists and two at her ankles. They were trying to give her a shot in her thigh to calm her down. She was wriggling out of their grasp and sliding down to the end of the bed. My then ninety-four-year-old mother was incredibly strong and putting up an incredible fight.

I started screaming, "Where is the doctor?" I needed both my mother to be different and the doctor to be there supervising this circus. It was then that one of the nurses took me aside to tell me that the seven-month-pregnant doctor had seen my mother as soon as she came in and my mother had proceeded to punch her in her very pregnant stomach. The doctor was not returning until my mother was sedated.

I felt like I was going to throw up.

And just when I thought things could not get any worse, my mother caught sight of me, and began yelling, "You are the worst daughter anyone could ever have. I hate you!"

That is when I turned around and walked out into the parking lot, listening the whole time to the small, scared voice inside of my head that was asking, "What do I do"?

I can remember, not too long ago, when that question would have paralyzed me for a long time with such an out-of-control fear.

Maybe that is how my mom feels when she is standing there in the parking lot and doesn't know what is happening and can't find any information in her mind to help her. Her mind is not functioning; she can't make sense of anything. She must feel so out of control.

My mind, at the moment I asked this question, was fully functioning. I was feeling out of control, but I knew how to answer my own question, "What do I do?" I knew how to stop feeling out of control.

In fact, I knew that it was within my control to stop feeling out of control.

I simply had to stop following my runaway mind, which was hurrying down into the pit of darkness where there was nothing but pain and misery and chaos and drama. And, as my mind was traveling in the wrong direction, it was picking up speed so that the story became bigger and juicier with each passing moment.

So, I refocused my mind, remembered not to take anything personally and accepted that this was happening.

This was my reality at the moment. Here was my mom doing exactly what she was doing and there I was, the daughter, feeling exactly what I was feeling. There was no alternate reality.

How I wanted to show up for myself and my mom became the focus of my attention and the question that I now was asking myself.

I walked back into the hospital.

I entered the room and saw the same bed, the same mother, the same men and the same voice yelling.

The only thing that had changed was my mind and that made all the difference in the world.

I was now traveling down a different path, one of my own choosing. I was no longer plummeting down the hole of despair. Everything was the same and yet everything was totally different.

I allowed what was, to be, which left me available to show up fully.

It took four shots to calm my mom down so they could test her to find out what was going on.

I have been hanging out in the world of dementia a lot lately. I am seeing that some of us may not have much longer with these pliant, moldable minds before we lose the ability to think on purpose and create what we want for ourselves by directing our minds.

Given that, just what do you want to do, while you can, with your one and only precious mind?

There is no time to waste here.

Birthday Musing

Jamie with her creation, 2010

It's my birthday today.

68 years on this planet Earth.

That's an amazing number of inhales and exhales since my very first breath into this life.

Yesterday, while I was driving home, I heard these lyrics to a song: "naked as we came."

We really did all come into this life naked.

We didn't arrive with things and attachments and stories.

We came in fresh and new.

What happens between that first breath and that last breath is all up for grabs.

I guess you could also say that what happens between my next 68-year-old breath and my last breath is up for grabs too.

It's not already written in stone, but rather it's created moment by moment.

It's where we put the focus of our attention.

It's what we claim to be important.

It's what we believe to be true.

So, on this day of my birth,

I honor and celebrate all of us.

Through some miracle of miracles, we breathed our way into this most spectacular adventure.

Let's not waste a second of it before we breathe our way out.

Drop all the armor, drop all the pretense, drop all the stories and become as naked as when you first arrived.

You were perfect then and you are still perfect now!

Sierra, California, 2019

Over the Rainbow

For weeks we have been struggling with the question:

"When will we know it is time to help our dog die so that we may ease her pain?"

We have been watching her like a hawk, making mental notes of what she ate, how she walked, any shifts that might mean she was heading downhill.

Yesterday morning I announced, "She's doing pretty well, she isn't going anywhere soon," as though I knew what the next moment would hold and I was actually in charge of the world.

So, in my mind, there was confusion when later in the day I clearly saw that she was in fact beginning the process of dying.

"Today? No not today!" my mind screamed.

Realizing there was nothing I could do to stop what had already been started and how little I knew about the mystery of life, I went to be with her and love her up for all her remaining moments until her very last breath.

As we drove her to the vet, me driving and my husband in the back cradling her, we had front row seats to one of the most spectacular sights of my lifetime - a double rainbow that made an arc in front of us, right over the road we were traveling on.

It was as though all three of us were heading straight into the center of the rainbow.

The sky was blazing with color.

Amazingly, there were no other cars on the road at all.

Just us, heading into the unknown.

I was awash with such joy at the beauty of this sight and, at the same time, flooded with so much sadness.

I wondered how I could hold such extreme emotions; joy and sorrow side by side.

And yet, there I was, doing just that, carrying the incredible fullness of life in my heart.

That is the way of it.

We are here in this life for the full ride.

I will be sad for my loss, but I will also be open to seeing the rainbows, as I know that both are part of the tapestry of life we are woven into and have the privilege to be part of.

Without the sad, I would never know about the immensity of the joy.

That is what our four-legged loves teach us, if we listen.

When we say yes to them, we say yes to the whole kit and caboodle of emotions.

What wonderful teachers they are.

So, to all furry ones everywhere, whether they are still in this life or they have already crossed over the rainbow,

I send out a deep, heartfelt, thank you, thank you, thank you.

My dog Bear, 15 years old, 2017

The Chocolate Story

My mom has always loved chocolate; chocolate anything. She would never turn down a chocolate staring her in the face.

For the past year or so I have been buying her boxes of chocolates at the grocery store so that she can share them with the nurses and anyone else she would care to share them with.

Since she has dementia, she is always surprised when I hold the box in front of her, open it and ask her if she would like a chocolate.

"Oh my, where did this come from? I just love chocolates," she always says as she helps herself to one or more.

One day, we were sitting in silence as she finished one of her chocolates and she turned to me and said, "You know, my mother drops these boxes of chocolates off here for me to eat."

I said, "Really? I didn't know that your mother came to visit. That is so nice of her to keep dropping off these boxes of chocolates for you!"

She said, "Yes. She feels so bad about what a mean mother she was to me. She is sorry for all those times she said NO, like no you can't do that, no you can't wear that, no you can't say that. She wants to make up for it, so she keeps bringing me chocolates. She knows I love them."

I sat there frozen for a moment.

This was amazing. My mother is 96 years old. Her mother is long dead. They had a terrible relationship, right up until my grandmother died 30 some years ago.

My mother was creating a new story. One that made her feel good. A story where her mother wasn't some terrible, awful woman trying to change and control her daughter while withholding her love.

This story made my mother happy.

What we think has such a powerful effect on not only ourselves but also those around us.

We don't have to be 96 with dementia in order to change those stories in our head that create pain and suffering for us. We are the creators of our own world by the perception we hold about everything from one moment to the next.

"My mother loves me," said my mom's new story as she took another bite of that sweet, delicious chocolate.

And I smiled, knowing without a shadow of a doubt that there is no piece of chocolate in the world that can ever taste as sweet as the power of knowing that we are always the author of our own story.

The Gift of Allowing

Lisa's Buddha, NH 2018

When I got word that the first snow was coming,
I was not pleased.

I had just gotten home from North Carolina, having
spent two weeks walking and riding my bike on the
beach every day.

I wanted flip-flop weather to last a bit longer,
which of course is a ridiculous thought to hold
onto if you live in the Northeast.

I felt like a child having a temper tantrum, standing
there in those flip-flops watching the snow falling
all around me.

"This is not what I want......whaaaaaaa!"

But the snow didn't listen.

Down it came and the flip-flops got relegated to the
back of the closet.

My life right now is here in the snow.

A few days after grudgingly shoveling the driveway,
and complaining about the cold, a friend shared a
photo with me.

It was the Buddha, sitting in the snow.

The Buddha was neither complaining or whining or
grudgingly wishing he could still wear his flip flops!

As I stared at this photo, the word that arose in my mind and my heart was

Allowing.

He was allowing the snow to land on him, gently and lovingly, receiving what was being offered.

"What a beautiful gift, this first snowfall.

Soft white fluff falling from the sky."

The photo asked me to change my opinion, to allow what was, instead of wishing it were different.

And from that place of allowing, a deep sense of calm arose, a calm that reminded me that all was well in my world.

The flip-flops were where they were supposed to be when you live in New England.

The snow was where it was supposed to be when you live in New Hampshire.

And I was exactly where I was supposed to be, right where I am.

Allowing all to be exactly as it is, is a beautiful thing.

The Buddha, holding space for it all, reminded me that nothing has gone wrong here.

We always have a choice about whether we receive what is being offered.

Right now,

I'm choosing to receive allowing as I watch the world sparkle every time a sunbeam caresses that freshly fallen snow.

The Stone House, NH 2013

Pep Talk to Myself

It seems to me

That

This girl is ALIVE in every fiber of her being.

She is pure joy.

She is surrendered into the moment.

She is grounded.

She is expansive.

She is being herself unapologetically.

She is inhabiting every cell of that little body and roaring out her strength from a place of fearlessness.

Today, I want to be this girl.

I want to channel her energy.

I want to be fearless and strong.

I am making a decision to do something that scares the bejeezus out of me.

If I am not careful and I don't manage my mind (which likes to keep me safe and tells me I am not strong enough and there is a lot to fear), I will just sit on the sidelines and wish I were that person who could do that thing and then silently and shrinkingly let my life and the opportunity pass me by.

I'm done with that way of thinking.

The only option left is to walk through the worst thing that can happen to me, which is feeling my own feelings of fear and anxiety.

And on the other side?

On the other side is this girl waiting for me out there
in the rain,
her arms stretched out to receive,
her feet planted in the pulse of the earth
and her mouth wide open
inviting me to join her as we both yell
at the top of our lungs,
YES!! YES!! YES!!

The Glory of Green

My mom, NH 2018

When I visit my mom, she is always lounging in the same chair in the corner of the same room.

It's her favorite chair because she gets to see all the goings-on.

She is like a queen on her throne.

Depending on her mood, she will be either telling everyone what to do, yelling for the nurses when someone needs assistance or has done something she thinks they shouldn't have, or resting quietly, eyes closed, taking one of those wonderful yummy naps full of fabulous far-away dreams.

But make no mistake, she is the hawk eye when she is awake and on the prowl.

When I go to see her on beautiful days, I will ask her if she wants to go outside.

The answer is always no.

Why would she want to move? She is so comfy where she is. It is so familiar. Why go into unknown territory? Her mind can't imagine something else, just right at this moment, in this corner.

Why change?

One of the nurses, in her infinite wisdom, showed me how not to ask but simply pull up a wheel chair or her walker and say, "Here, let me help you up. I have something amazing to show you."

It works every time.

Who doesn't want to see something amazing? Maybe it is also the energy in my voice, the excitement that I muster for that amazingness to come that I can't wait for her to see.

So, on this particular day, we go outside for a walk with my brother and my daughter. It is indeed amazingly gorgeous out. We all slow ourselves down for the beauty.

But none of us as much as my mother. She acts as if she is in a 3D movie with her special glasses on. It is the big, wide world in technicolor.

Her world has been shrunk to her little living quarters, which she feels comfortable in, but this wide-open space, this full-life production of nature and aliveness - this is something else altogether.

We stop for a break to admire and rest. She crosses her legs, looks all around and then with a smile on her face, reaches her arms up to the heavens and announces in the loudest voice she can muster,

"LOOK AT ALL THIS GREEN!"

All of our heads look up and, sure enough, everything is green and enormous and vivid... it's life pulsing in that moment.

And I want to reach my arms up and yell, "Look at you Mom, a sight I never thought I would see in my life." My mom, sitting here in wild abandon without a care in the world, is rejoicing as though she has never experienced any of this in her 97 years on this earth.

It was a hallelujah moment for sure.

And that is the thing.

It's all in a moment. Everything, every little thing, happens moment to moment.

We have so many moments of amazement and expansiveness. We just need to be present for them when they arise.

And when you are present enough to meet the moment, be sure to raise your arms up high and let yourself be filled with the pulse of life as it comes tumbling in through your outstretched arms.

You're never too old to live full out in technicolor.

Stepping into my Name

I love synchronicities.

In the morning, I was standing on the dock out at Nubanusit Lake looking at the glorious Morning Star in the sky while watching the new day beginning to unfold before my eyes.

In the afternoon, I was in the bank where a teller I have never seen before greeted me with a big smile and a "so glad to see you Janet."

I asked her if we had met and she said, "Only through your transactions. I'm usually your drive-up teller and I know you because you are the Morningstar."

"I was the Morningstar." I loved the sound of that.

What she was referring to was the name on my checks. Janet Morningstar Archer.

I was not always a Morningstar.

I did not have a cool, free-spirited mother who named me in some meaningful way.

In fact, I never thought my mother had put much thought into my name at all. The story she told me was that I was named after her roommate in the hospital, whom she had just met after I was born. For years I believed that my mom must not have loved me very much to have named me after her hospital roommate.

Believing that story was painful and I know exactly when I made the decision to stop believing it was true.

It was after my mom told me her own painful story, the one that her mother had told her. In that story, my grandmother told my mom she had brought the wrong baby home from the hospital, and that my mother really wasn't her child.

And that is how it came to pass that at the age of 43, I took on the role of mending the flow of faulty thinking that was running rampant down the matriarchal lineage of my family tree.

I made the decision to name myself Morningstar.

I had just gotten divorced and I wanted to create a new start with a new name.

I wanted a name that sounded strong and bold.

A name that signified, in my mind, that I was going to make it and be OK.

The Morningstar was bright and expansive.
It ushered in each day and signaled the beginning of a new life to me.

I wanted that - a name filled with hope and deliberateness.

About that time, my dad was growing concerned about this Morningstar business.

"I hope you are not going to give yourself one of those ridiculous hippie names," he kept saying to me.

I was not giving up Morningstar.

I started pouring through old names from my grandmother's side of the family and after much searching I found the perfect name: Archer. It had been my grandmother's mother's maiden name.

The Archer took aim and moved forward, no matter what.

Janet Ann Young to Janet Morningstar Archer.

This was probably one of the most empowered things I ever did up to that point in my life and also one of the scariest.

The voices in my head were screaming.

"Who do you think you are? You can't rename yourself! You can't choose what you want! You can't make things up out of thin air. You can't!"

But the truth is I could and I did. I didn't let those voices in my head stop me.

When I went to the court to legally change my name, I was sure the judge was going to laugh at me and tell me how ridiculous I was being.

But all he did was ask me if I was sure this is what I wanted to do.

Over the next months, I would ask myself several times, "Who the heck is this Janet Morningstar Archer?" But after a while, I began to step more and more fully into my new name.

I had forgotten how important naming myself was to me until last week when I saw the Morning Star in the sky and spoke to the teller at the bank.

You can do a lot of things that your mind tells you can't be done. I know, because I have.

Today is a new day.

And I for one am heading out into it, blazing like the Morning Star and taking aim at what I want like the Archer.

May I never forget who I decided to be!

Me on top of Bald Mt, NH 2018

The Rush

There is no rush.

I hear those words but I don't quite believe them.

I live as though there is a rush.

I go to see my mom about every other day. I am usually rushing to get there. I add the trip on to something I was just doing or something that I will be doing after I visit with her. She is usually sandwiched in between because my belief is that it saves me time.

Saves me time for what, I wonder?

When I visit her, we sit or walk.

There is no rush when I am there.

I rush to get there, take a moment of no rushing when I am there and then rush away to something else.

That is pretty much how my day looks. Rush, don't rush, rush, don't rush. And sometimes there is a rush, rush, rush with no stopping for the no-rush part. Then there is drop-down, flat-out exhaustion.

Something I have been practicing saying to myself is,

"There is no better there than here!"

Driving in my car, between here and there, believing that there is something better than being right here driving in my car while going there, I stop to remember,

"There is no better there than here."

With that thought in mind, I begin to feel my hands on the steering wheel, hear the hum of the engine and relax my shoulders, my jaw and my brain.

When I am with my mom, I stop to remember,

"There is no better there than here."

Thinking that thought drops me into a space of being present while I hold her hand, rub her back, sit there with her, words or no words, not thinking that something is better than this.

Typing these words while sitting on my front porch, wanting the words to be done so I can move on to the next thing, I remember,

"There is no better there than here."

That's when I begin feeling my fingers on the keyboard, the breeze on my skin and the sound of the leaves in the trees.

It's a practice.

My mind wants to rush ahead; it wants me to believe that where I am is not the place to be.

But when I stop to practice "there is no better there than here" I feel the weight of all the rushing begin to fall off my body, slide down my arms, flow out of my fingers and I begin to S L O W down and arrive here.

I promise you

there is no rush.

We have all the time in the world to be here, when there is no thought brewing in our minds that where we are is not where we are supposed to be.

A Bunch of Crazy

Any time I go anywhere, there is always someone who asks me when I am going to write another story about my mom.

I tell my mom that she is famous and she just laughs and says, "Isn't that nice."

Today I had lunch with her.

She lives in a lock down unit so you have to put a code in the key pad to get in.

She used to ask me what the code was so she could get in and out herself.

I would always tell her, knowing that she would never remember past the moment I told her.

She doesn't ask anymore, nor does she show any interest in getting out. I believe she knows that she is in and that everyone who enters comes from the out.

Sometimes when I walk in, I feel like I walk into another world altogether.

If I, at all, wanted my mom to be different, it would be really hard to enter this world.

Today, at lunch, there was a woman eating at a table outside my mother's room. She pointed her out to me and said, "You see that old lady over there? Well, she has come in from the forest and we put some food out there on our patio for her every day so she will have something to eat."

"That is interesting," I say.

One of the nurses, who loves to sing to everyone, had made a make-believe microphone headset and attached two cups to her waist. On one cup it said, TO KEEP ME SINGING. On the other cup it said TO SHUT ME UP. She gave out poker chips so you could put chips in the cup you wanted to vote for. I was throwing those chips in the cups with vigor, as was my mom.

So much fun.

So much laughter.

So much lightness.

And then, my mom leans over and whispers to me, "When you walk through that door, you just find a bunch of crazy in here!"

She had a big old smile on her face as she said it.

Yes, total crazy.

But what I also thought at that moment was that when you punched yourself out to the other side of the door, there was crazy out there as well.

It's so fascinating that I get mad at the crazy over on my side of the door but not on my mom's side of the door.

I wondered about the difference.

I think the answer for me is that I expect it on her side and I don't expect it on mine.

I fight with reality on my side, but I don't on her side.

We're all living in a delusion that things shouldn't be the way they are.

All I know is that when I am not demanding that

there is no woman living in a forest being fed

outside of what my mom calls her house,

and I am not demanding that the weather should
not be this cold

and I am not demanding that people should act

differently,

then I can relax

and let life be as it is,

which includes the crazy,

on both sides of the door.

Delight

Me, Sunset Beach, NC 2017

Too many times over the last few weeks I have noticed my mind thinking thoughts that would never create the feeling of delight.

So, the other day as I was riding my bike on the beach, I asked my husband to take a photo of me as I was smack dab in the middle of feeling delight.

Delight of being one of the only people on the beach

delight of riding into the sunset

delight of the air caressing my skin

delight of the sound of my tires rolling through the wet sand

delight of the waves crashing around me

delight of the smell and spray of the ocean air

delight of my mind thinking thoughts that were bringing delight

delight of my husband being there to take my photo

delight of sharing this moment with him

delight that my hamstring injury seemed to love the action of peddling the bike

delight that I had thought to buy this bike

delight that it is pink

delight that it was the day before Thanksgiving and I was where I was.

And finally, delight that I gave to myself what I most needed:

an afternoon of sheer delight.

So delightful!

The Christmas Police

Christmas, 2016

The way my mind is carrying on, you would think there was really such a thing as the Christmas police.

You know, they knock on your door any time after mid-January to check and see if your Christmas decorations are down.

Then what they'll do when they see reds and greens and twinkling lights all around, I haven't a clue!

"It's way past time to take those decorations down," they might demand.

But at my house, they will be yelling at a person who doesn't want to listen. She doesn't want to "obey the law."

She's not ready to take the decorations down yet.

She is still enjoying them, and as far as she can see, those decorations aren't harming anyone.

The funny (or not so funny) thing is that we all live with the police knocking at the door of our minds all the time.

"Do this, do that, this is not right, this is all wrong."

Personally, I like to practice challenging those laws.

"Why do my decorations have to come down now? Who says so?

What does it mean about me if I leave them up? Do I really need to be arrested?

What is it that I really want to do and why don't I listen to that instead of those police running around in my mind?"

I'm just not ready to take those decorations down yet.

Stop by if you want. Have a look around and tell all your friends that I still have my decorations up.

Call the police. I'm not scared,

because if they should arrive,

I'm ready.

I'll sit them down by the warm fire,

put their tired feet up on the foot rest,

turn on all the twinkling lights

and then I'll serve them an eggnog or two.

No arrests will be happening at this house,

just another sweet, still night

where all is well

and all is most definitely right.

Just Laugh

I was teaching a chair yoga dance class this morning to some wonderful women who live in an assisted living facility.

I taught them the basic moves and then before I put the music on, I told them that if they got mixed up and either forgot or couldn't get their body part to move to the place that they were directing it to, then they should just laugh.

For 45 minutes I was on the receiving end of the glow from these beautiful, smiling, vibrant, joyful faces that were following my directions

to just laugh,

just have fun

for the sheer pleasure of it.

Laughter is the sweetest medicine;

it doesn't cost a penny and you can find it anywhere.

Seek some out today or, better yet, create some of your own

and then watch everything around you

radiate and bloom,

as the world responds to the

lightness

of the person called you.

Frannie Got the Last Word

My mom, Hawaii, 2010

I was waiting for the end of the book to come to me. Not really sitting around and waiting, but being aware that the ending was looking for me and that I needed to keep a look out for it.

What I love is that the ending of my book came from my mom, Frannie, whom you have gotten to know through these stories.

Every time I visit her, she wants me to stay for lunch. She yells into the kitchen, "Set an extra place; my daughter is here." Many times, she offers to pay the check. One time, she insisted on paying for the meal. So, one of the nurses gave her a make-believe check on a napkin and she was satisfied with the transaction.

One day, six of us were sitting around a table in the kitchen. My mom had just been served her plate of food and was slowly eating. I was next to her sipping a cup of soup. A nurse was next to me feeding someone who needed assistance. Next to them was a husband helping his wife eat.

My mom stopped eating, looked around the table and started waving her arm as though she were encircling all of us.

She said, "This is quite some table!"

The nurse, the husband and I all waited to hear what she would say next. Anything goes with her. When she talks, she can go in the direction of either being incredibly rude or surprisingly kind.

Her announcement was followed by silence, so I asked her what she meant, "Why is this quite some table mom?"

Her arm began circling us all with the gesture again, and then she said,

"We are all just temporary!"

Not at all what I was expecting. But in my mind, I believed something profound had just been uttered.

Nothing will ever happen exactly the same again.

Each of us is a traveler on this planet world that is spinning a zillion miles an hour out in the immensity of space.

We all have a seat at the table and, yes, it is quite some table.

Your place and my place have been set with the bounty of our lives piled high on our plates.

The invitation that we were all born with is to remember that we are here for such a short visit,

such a fleeting moment in time.

It also invites each of us to pause and partake fully because, before too long,

our plate will be removed

and the table cleared.

This is it.

This is our blink in time.

Frannie, as always, got the last word.

She would be happy about that.

This is all just temporary.

In Gratitude

A huge shout out of love and gratitude to everyone who helped bring this book to life: my family, my friends, my clients, my students, my teachers, my coaches, my book team, everyone who has ever read a word I have written, and to all of you who are reading my words for the very first time, a deep, heartfelt, thank you.

Photo Credits